OUR PLANET THE
Earth

Writer: Keith Lye
Designer: Tri-Art
Illustrators: Max Ansell, Gordon Davies,
Roger Full Associates, Angela Heaseman,
Duncan Mill, Pat Mynot, Lee Noel, Geoff Taylor
Cover Illustrator: Derek Bunce
Series Editor: Christopher Tunney
Art Director: Keith Groom

LIBRARY OF CONGRESS CATALOGING IN PUBLICATION DATA

Lye, Keith.
Our planet the earth.

(The Question and answer books)
Includes index.
SUMMARY: Presents questions and answers about the planet
earth, its composition, and the forces which are constantly
changing it.

1. Earth sciences—Juvenile literature. [1. Earth sciences. 2.
Questions and answers] I. Ansell, Max. II. Title. III. Title:
Earth.

QE29.L93   1980   550   79-2346
ISBN 0-8225-1182-7   lib. bdg.

The Question and Answer Books

OUR PLANET THE
Earth

 Lerner Publications Company ▪ Minneapolis

How did ancient peoples see the world?

PLANET EARTH Early peoples based many of their ideas about the Earth on superstitions. But we now understand that the Earth is a planet in the solar system, which is rotating around the center of the Milky Way galaxy. The Earth also rotates around the Sun, at the same time spinning on its own axis. Day and night occur alternately as part of the Earth faces the Sun and is then turned away from it. And, because the Earth's axis is tilted, we have seasons.

From Hindu legends, we know that Indians once thought that the Earth looked like the drawing above. They thought that the Earth rested on a golden plate supported by elephants. The elephants stood on a turtle, representing the water god, Vishnu.

Where is the Earth in the solar system?

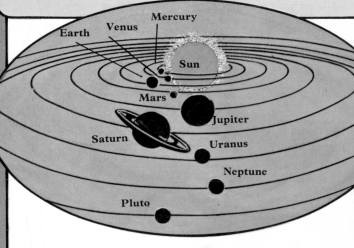

The Earth is the third planet from the Sun. Only Mercury and Venus are closer to the Sun. Apart from the nine planets, the solar system also contains moons, meteorites, comets, asteroids, gas, and dust.

What is the Earth's axis?

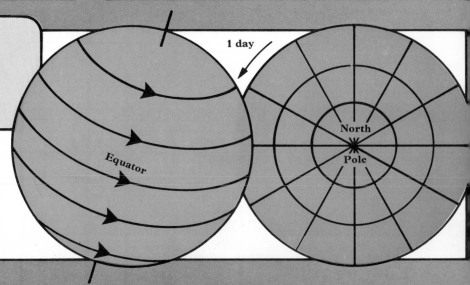

The Earth's axis is an imaginary line joining the North Pole, the center of the Earth, and the South Pole. The axis is tilted at $66\frac{1}{2}°$ to the plane of the Earth's orbit. The average time taken by the Earth to spin once on its axis is about 24 hours, or one complete day.

Is time the same everywhere on Earth?

On Earth, 15° of longitude represents 1 hour's time difference, because 15° × 24 hours equals 360°—the number of degrees in a circle. Time zones are modified to prevent a small country having two times.

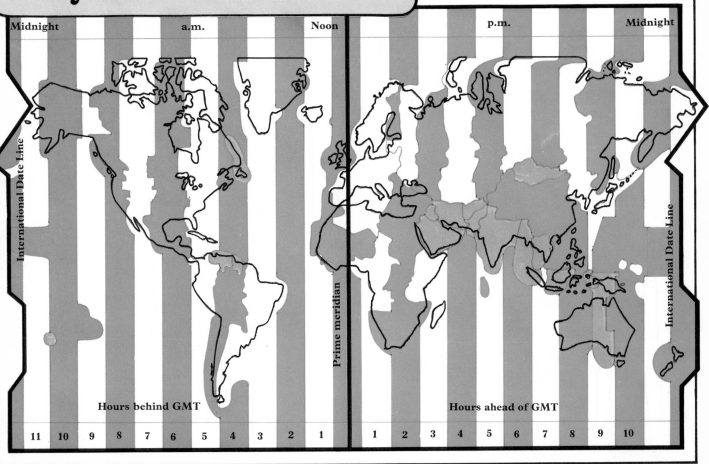

Midnight				a.m.					Noon					p.m.						Midnight

International Date Line

Prime meridian

International Date Line

Hours behind GMT

Hours ahead of GMT

11	10	9	8	7	6	5	4	3	2	1		1	2	3	4	5	6	7	8	9	10

Why are there seasons?

Spring equinox
N. Hemisphere
Autumn equinox
S. Hemisphere
March 21

Summer solstice
N. Hemisphere
Winter solstice
S. Hemisphere
June 21

Winter solstice
N. Hemisphere
Summer solstice
S. Hemisphere
December 21

Autumn equinox
N. Hemisphere
Spring equinox
S. Hemisphere
September 23

At the equinoxes, the Sun is overhead at the Equator. It is overhead at the Tropic of Cancer (23°27′N) or the Tropic of Capricorn (23°27′S) at the solstices. This changing position of the overhead Sun explains why we have seasons.

5

How was the solar system formed?

Most scientists think that, 5,000 million years ago, our Solar System was a mass of gas and dust (top). This material contracted to form the Sun (center) and the planets (bottom) about 4,550 million years ago.

THE EARTH WE LIVE ON Our planet Earth was formed about 4,550 million years ago, probably from a cloud of gas and dust that was drifting around the newly created Sun. As the Earth formed, heavier materials, such as iron, sank toward the core. Lighter materials rose and hardened to form the thin crust. Today, oceans cover more than seven-tenths of the Earth's surface. But the land is extremely varied, from mountain ranges to plains.

What is the Earth's interior like?

Facts and Figures About the Earth
Size The diameter of the Earth at the Equator is 7,926 miles (12,756 km). But the Earth is not a true sphere. The diameter from pole to pole is 7,899 miles (12,713 km).
Mass 5,882 million million million tons.
Area 196,937,600 sq miles (510,066,000 sq km).
Land Area About 29 per cent of the Earth's surface.
Highest peak on land Everest, 29,028 feet (8,848 m) above sea level.
Water area About 71 per cent of the Earth's surface.
Deepest point in the oceans 36,198 feet (11,033 m) in the Marianas Trench, in the Pacific Ocean. The deepest descent was 35,820 feet (10,918 m) in 1960.
Highest recorded air temperature 136.4°F (58.0°C), in Libya in 1922.
Lowest recorded air temperature—126.9°F (−88.3°C), recorded in Antarctica (1960).

Crust

Inner core

Outer core

Mantle

The Earth's crust is only a thin shell, between 4 and 37 miles (6 and 60 km) thick. Beneath the crust is the dense mantle, which is 1,800 miles (2,900 km) thick. The core's diameter is about 4,300 miles (6,920 km). The outer core is liquid, but the extremely dense inner core is solid.

How much of the Earth is covered by water?

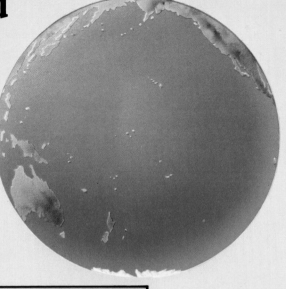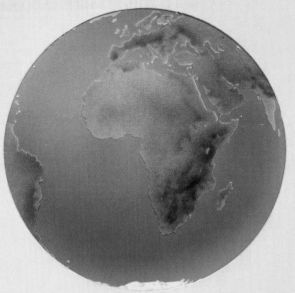

These two views of the Earth show how much of its surface is covered by water. The land hemisphere has its center between London and Berlin. The sea hemisphere has its center near New Zealand.

Which is the highest mountain?

What is the highest point on land?

The highest point in the world is Mount Everest, in the Himalayas. It rises to a height of 29,028 feet (8,848 m) above sea level, on the borders of Nepal and Tibet, north of India. The Himalayan range has several peaks higher than 23,000 feet (7,000 m). It is known as the "Roof of the World."

What is the lowest point on land?

The Dead Sea is an extremely salty lake between Israel and Jordan. Because it is so salty, people can float in it without sinking. The shore of the Dead Sea is the lowest point on land anywhere in the world. It is 1,289 feet (393 m) lower than the mean sea level of the Mediterranean Sea, which lies to the west.

We usually think of Mount Everest as the world's highest mountain. However, some volcanic peaks rise from the sea bed and surface as islands. One of them, Mauna Kea, in Hawaii, is 33,474 feet (10,203 m) high—measured from the ocean bed. But only 13,796 feet (4,205 m) is actually above sea level.

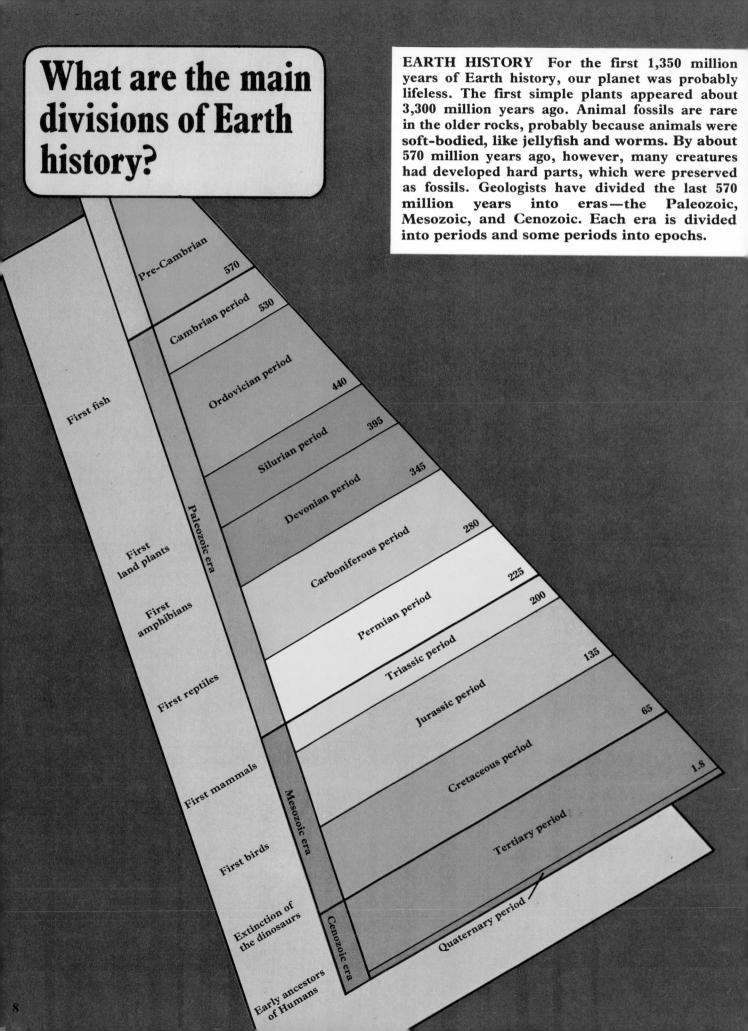

What are the main divisions of Earth history?

EARTH HISTORY For the first 1,350 million years of Earth history, our planet was probably lifeless. The first simple plants appeared about 3,300 million years ago. Animal fossils are rare in the older rocks, probably because animals were soft-bodied, like jellyfish and worms. By about 570 million years ago, however, many creatures had developed hard parts, which were preserved as fossils. Geologists have divided the last 570 million years into eras—the Paleozoic, Mesozoic, and Cenozoic. Each era is divided into periods and some periods into epochs.

First fish

First land plants

First amphibians

First reptiles

First mammals

First birds

Extinction of the dinosaurs

Early ancestors of Humans

Paleozoic era

Mesozoic era

Cenozoic era

Pre-Cambrian 570

Cambrian period 530

Ordovician period 440

Silurian period 395

Devonian period 345

Carboniferous period 280

Permian period 225

Triassic period 200

Jurassic period 135

Cretaceous period 65

Tertiary period 1.8

Quaternary period

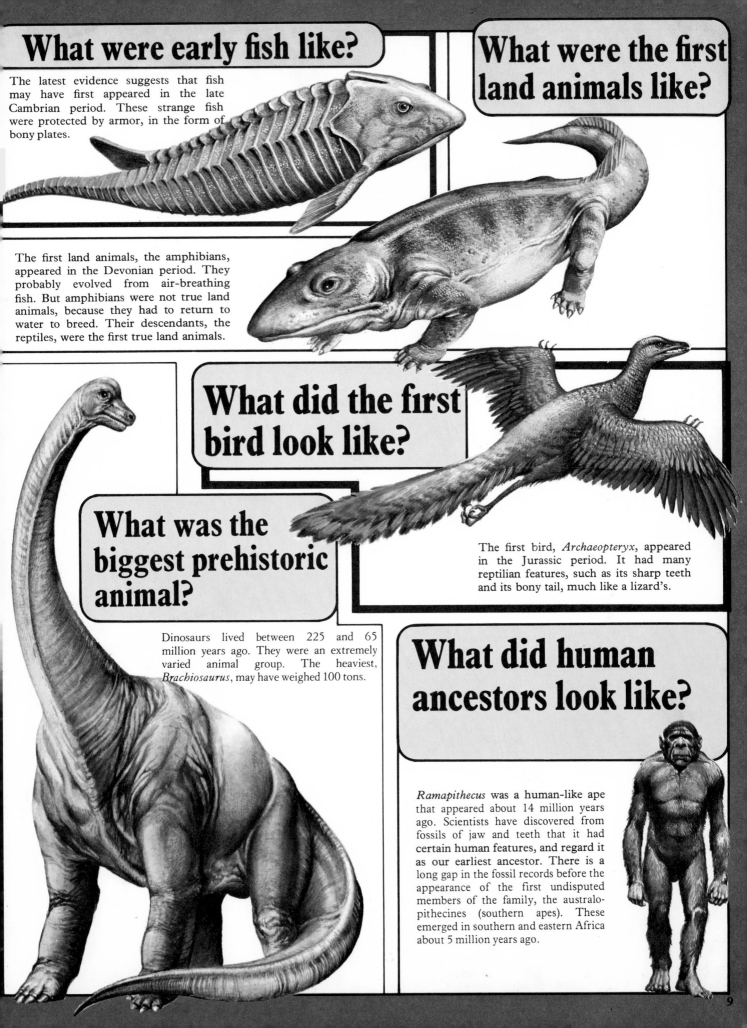

What were early fish like?

The latest evidence suggests that fish may have first appeared in the late Cambrian period. These strange fish were protected by armor, in the form of bony plates.

What were the first land animals like?

The first land animals, the amphibians, appeared in the Devonian period. They probably evolved from air-breathing fish. But amphibians were not true land animals, because they had to return to water to breed. Their descendants, the reptiles, were the first true land animals.

What did the first bird look like?

The first bird, *Archaeopteryx*, appeared in the Jurassic period. It had many reptilian features, such as its sharp teeth and its bony tail, much like a lizard's.

What was the biggest prehistoric animal?

Dinosaurs lived between 225 and 65 million years ago. They were an extremely varied animal group. The heaviest, *Brachiosaurus*, may have weighed 100 tons.

What did human ancestors look like?

Ramapithecus was a human-like ape that appeared about 14 million years ago. Scientists have discovered from fossils of jaw and teeth that it had certain human features, and regard it as our earliest ancestor. There is a long gap in the fossil records before the appearance of the first undisputed members of the family, the australo-pithecines (southern apes). These emerged in southern and eastern Africa about 5 million years ago.

What happens where the continents meet the oceans?

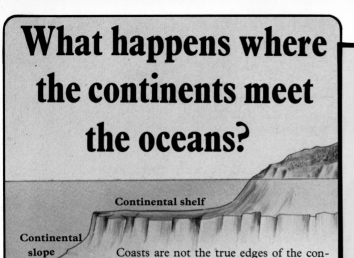

Coasts are not the true edges of the continents. Beyond the coasts is a shallow, gently sloping continental shelf, which is part of the continent. The continent really ends where the continental slope plunges steeply down to the oceanic abyss.

DRIFTING CONTINENTS The ground under our feet may seem firm. But it is actually moving, although the movement is slow. The Earth's crust is divided into several large areas, called "plates," which are separated by huge cracks. These plates move in two main ways. In places, hot, fluid mantle rock beneath the plates is rising and spreading, moving the plates along. And new rock is being added to the crust along underwater mountain ranges, called mid-oceanic ridges. This steady addition of new rock is pushing apart the plates on either side.

What is a plate?

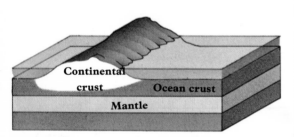

The plates in the Earth's crust are made up of the thin ocean crust and the continents that rest upon it. Beneath the ocean crust is the dense mantle. The top of the mantle is partly fluid. Currents in this fluid rock make the plates move.

Were the continents always separate?

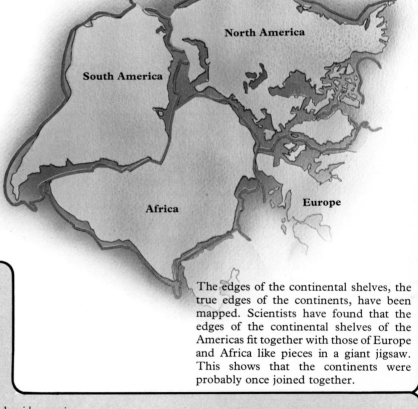

The edges of the continental shelves, the true edges of the continents, have been mapped. Scientists have found that the edges of the continental shelves of the Americas fit together with those of Europe and Africa like pieces in a giant jigsaw. This shows that the continents were probably once joined together.

Does the sea bed show evidence of continental drift?

In the oceans, there are huge mountain ranges called *mid-oceanic ridges*. Scientists have discovered that new rock is being added along the center of these ridges. As a result, the oceans are being widened.

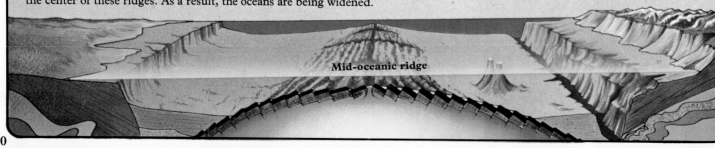

Is there any other evidence?

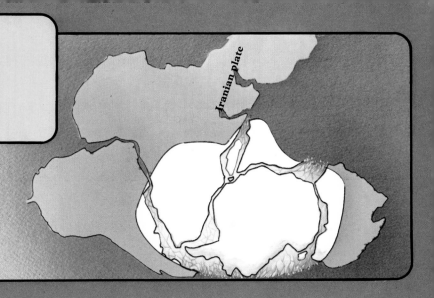

About 290 million years ago, there was a great Ice Age in the Southern Hemisphere. Studies of this Ice Age suggest that the continents were then joined, as the map shows. Fossils of the same animals and plants occur in the continents. This evidence also supports the theory.

What are the chief plates in the Earth's crust?

Below: Four views of the Earth show the main plates in the Earth's crust. Some of these plates are enormous, but some are fairly small. The plates are moving slowly. Near their edges are unstable areas, where volcanoes and earthquakes occur.

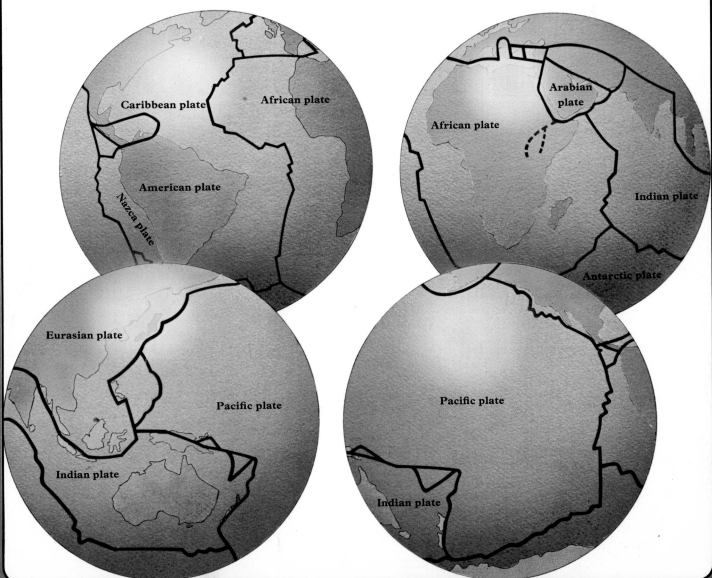

How did the continents move apart?

CONTINENTS COLLIDE The plates in the crusts are moving by about three-fourths inch (2 cm) or less per year. But this movement has been going on for hundreds of millions of years. As a result, the continents have drifted apart over 200 million years. In places where plates are pushing against each other, crustal rock is being destroyed as one plate is pushed under the other. Sometimes, when two plates collide, the sediments between them are squeezed up into fold mountains.

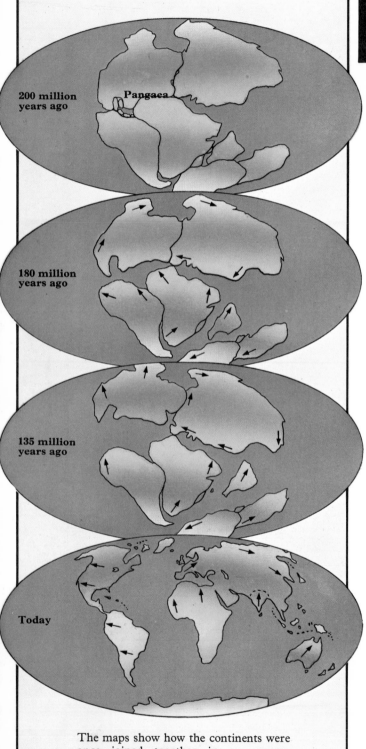

200 million years ago — Pangaea

180 million years ago

135 million years ago

Today

The maps show how the continents were once joined together in one super-continent, Pangaea, about 200 million years ago. But Pangaea split up and the land masses drifted slowly to their present positions.

What makes plates drift?

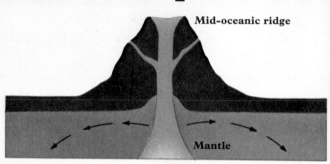

Mid-oceanic ridge

Mantle

The diagram shows molten rock rising to the surface along the mid-oceanic ridges. There it hardens and becomes new crustal rock. This widens the oceans. The diagram also shows currents in the mantle, which spread sideways, pushing the plates apart.

What are folds?

Evidence of the tremendous forces at work inside the Earth is shown in folded rocks. These rocks were formed in flat layers. But great lateral (sideways) pressure occurs when plates push against each other. The flat layers of rock are squeezed into great loops or folds.

What happens when plates collide?

When two plates push against each other, the edge of one plate is sometimes forced under the other. The descending plate edge is melted. Some of the melted rock may return to the surface through volcanoes.

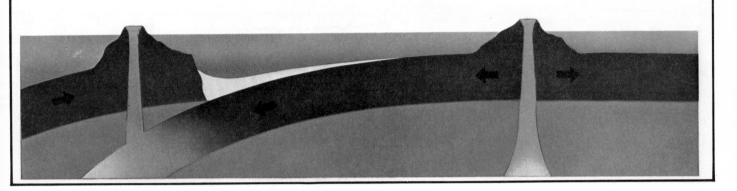

Does anything else happen?

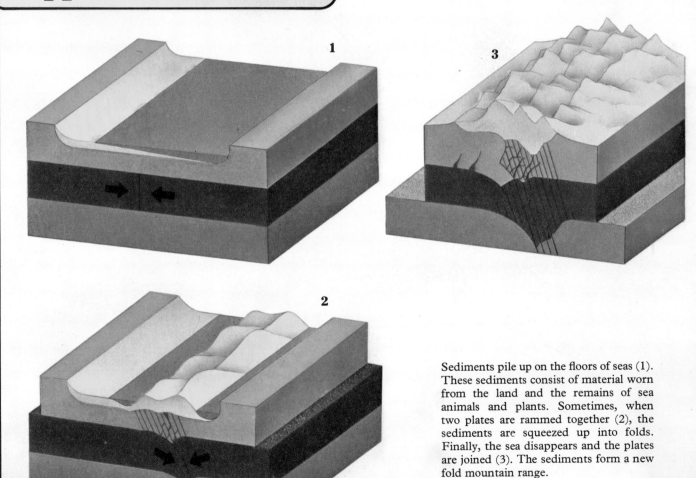

Sediments pile up on the floors of seas (1). These sediments consist of material worn from the land and the remains of sea animals and plants. Sometimes, when two plates are rammed together (2), the sediments are squeezed up into folds. Finally, the sea disappears and the plates are joined (3). The sediments form a new fold mountain range.

What is a fault?

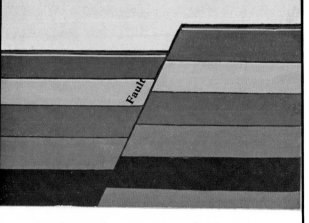

Faults are fractures, or cracks, in rock layers along which the rocks have moved. The movement is usually up and down, as shown above. After movement has occurred, the rock layers on either side of the fault do not match.

MOUNTAIN BUILDING Apart from fold mountains, there are two other main kinds of mountains. Block mountains are blocks of land that have been pushed up between faults in the Earth's crust. Volcanoes are mostly found near the edges of the crust's plates. Volcanoes are sometimes steep cones of volcanic ash. Others are lower but broader and are composed of layer upon layer of hardened lava. Some consist of alternate layers of ash and lava.

How are block mountains and rift valleys formed?

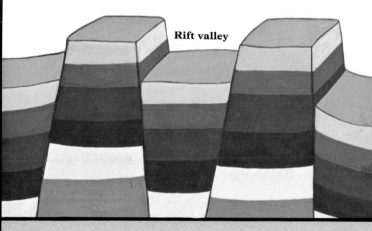

Block mountain

Rift valley

Vertical movements along faults create such features as block mountains, which are uplifted blocks of land, and rift valleys, where a block of land has slipped down between the faults. Small block mountains, which form ridges, are called *horsts*.

What are the main kinds of rock folds?

A simple up-fold in rocks is called an *anticline*. A simple down-fold is called a *syncline*. Some up-folds, such as the one on the left, contain many smaller folds. This complicated fold is called an *anticlinorium*. A *nappe* is a fold that has been bent over, broken away, and pushed along.

Anticlinorium

Anticline

Syncline

Nappe

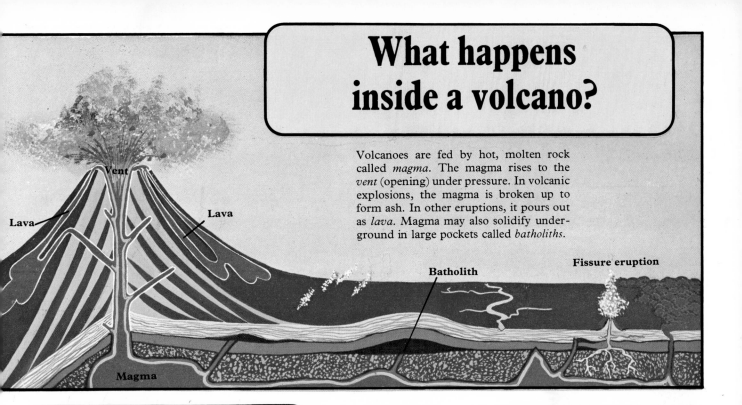

What happens inside a volcano?

Volcanoes are fed by hot, molten rock called *magma*. The magma rises to the *vent* (opening) under pressure. In volcanic explosions, the magma is broken up to form ash. In other eruptions, it pours out as *lava*. Magma may also solidify underground in large pockets called *batholiths*.

What is lava like?

Lava is a terrifying sight as it advances toward a town. People have tried to cool and harden the lava by pumping water on it. But there is no real way of stopping its advance. People must wait until the eruption ends, and hope that their homes have not been destroyed by the lava.

VOLCANIC ERUPTIONS Some volcanoes erupt explosively. The lava inside the volcano and, sometimes, parts of the mountain itself, are shattered by explosive gases. Small pieces of hot volcanic ash or dust are shot into the air. They then rain down on surrounding areas, burning and burying fields and towns. In volcanoes where there is little gas, the eruptions are "quiet"—that is, streams of lava are emitted, but there is no explosion. Most volcanoes are intermediate, sometimes erupting explosively and sometimes quietly. Other features of volcanic regions are hot springs and geysers.

Do volcanoes contribute to life on Earth?

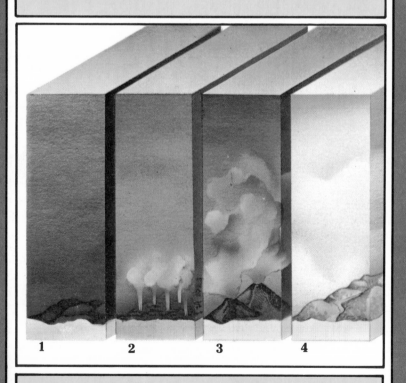

1   2   3   4

Volcanic action releases gases from the Earth's rocks. The first atmosphere (1), which was later lost into space, was created from the molten surface of the newly formed Earth. A new atmosphere was formed from lava and volcanoes (2 and 3). Then plants added oxygen, producing the mixture of air we breathe today (4).

Are there many kinds of volcanic eruptions?

Top: Quiet volcanoes, such as those in Hawaii, are shaped like an upturned saucer. They emit lava and do not explode. *Center:* Explosive volcanoes are typified by Mt. Vesuvius in Italy, which erupted in AD 79. *Bottom: A nuée ardente,* or *glowing cloud* of hot gases, steam, and ash, is a feature of some volcanic explosions.

What were the effects of the famous Krakatoa eruption?

Krakatoa, a volcanic island between Java and Sumatra, was destroyed in 1883 by a great volcanic explosion. The sound was heard in Australia, thousands of miles away. Ash rained down on surrounding islands, which were also battered by a destructive wave, or *tsunami*.

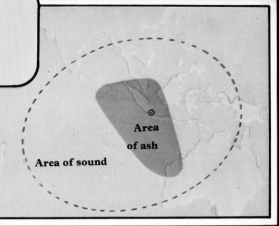

Area of ash

Area of sound

Do volcanoes ever form new land?

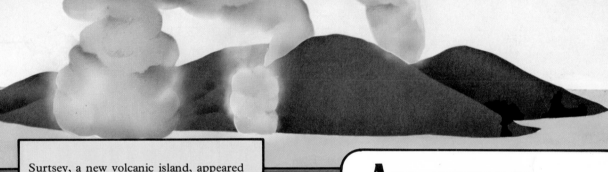

Surtsey, a new volcanic island, appeared off Iceland in 1963. It rose from the mid-Atlantic ridge. Three weeks after it had surfaced, Surtsey was 400 feet (120 meters) high and nearly 0·6 mile (1 km) across.

Are geysers connected with volcanoes?

Has a volcano ever buried an entire city?

Pompeii was a Roman town near the Bay of Naples, in Italy. In AD 79, the town was buried by hot ash and pumice which came from the explosive eruption of nearby Mt. Vesuvius. It lay hidden for hundreds of years, but much of it has now been excavated.

Geysers are types of hot springs that periodically erupt jets of hot water and steam into the air. They sometimes occur because underground water is heated to steam by magma in volcanic regions. The steam forces the water upward. Other geyser eruptions are caused by gases in the water.

What causes earthquakes?

EARTHQUAKES Most earthquakes are caused by rocks moving along faults. Earthquakes can occur anywhere. But they are most common and most severe near plate edges. The place where an earthquake originates is the focus, which is usually underground. The point on the surface directly above it is the epicenter. The strength of earthquakes is measured on the Richter scale, which is numbered from 1 to 9. A 2-point quake is barely noticeable. But a 7-point quake is severe.

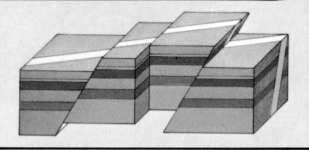

The movement along most faults is vertical. But movements may occur in any direction. For example, movements along some faults are horizontal—that is, the rocks move alongside each other. It is the sudden movements at faults that cause earthquakes.

Why is the San Andreas fault famous?

The San Andreas fault is in California, near the cities of Los Angeles and San Francisco. The fault is about 597 miles (960 km) long. It forms part of the boundary between the Pacific plate, which is moving north-westwards, and the American plate, which is moving south-eastwards.

What is the greatest disaster caused by the San Andreas fault?

Movements along the San Andreas fault are not smooth. The jagged edges of the plates become jammed together. The pressure then builds up until the jam breaks and the rocks lurch suddenly forward. A sudden movement in 1906 caused the San Francisco earthquake. Near the city, the fault moved 15 feet (4.6 meters).

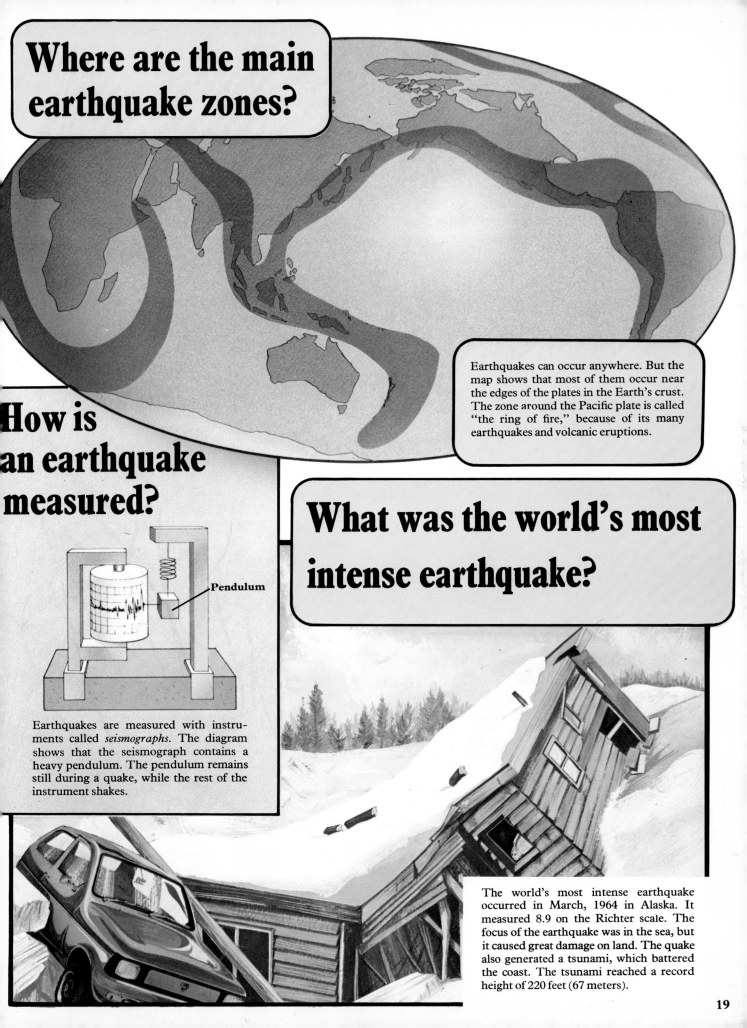

Where are the main earthquake zones?

Earthquakes can occur anywhere. But the map shows that most of them occur near the edges of the plates in the Earth's crust. The zone around the Pacific plate is called "the ring of fire," because of its many earthquakes and volcanic eruptions.

How is an earthquake measured?

Pendulum

Earthquakes are measured with instruments called *seismographs*. The diagram shows that the seismograph contains a heavy pendulum. The pendulum remains still during a quake, while the rest of the instrument shakes.

What was the world's most intense earthquake?

The world's most intense earthquake occurred in March, 1964 in Alaska. It measured 8.9 on the Richter scale. The focus of the earthquake was in the sea, but it caused great damage on land. The quake also generated a tsunami, which battered the coast. The tsunami reached a record height of 220 feet (67 meters).

ROCKS Rocks formed from molten magma are called igneous rocks. They include basalt and granite. Rocks that form from worn fragments of other rocks are called sedimentary rocks. They are so called because they mostly form as sediments in water. Sedimentary rocks include sandstones and shales. They often contain fossils, which are evidence of ancient life. Rocks that have been changed by heat, pressure, or chemical action are called metamorphic rocks.

How much sedimentary rock is there in the upper part of the Earth's crust?

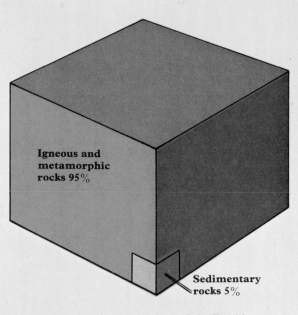

Igneous and metamorphic rocks 95%

Sedimentary rocks 5%

In the top 10 miles (16 km) of the Earth's crust, 95 per cent of the rocks are either igneous or metamorphic. Only five per cent are sedimentary. But sedimentary rocks are the commonest on the surface.

How much of the Earth's land surface is covered by sedimentary rock?

Sedimentary rocks 75%

Igneous and metamorphic rocks 25%

The most common rocks exposed on the Earth's surface are sedimentary rocks. These rocks are formed mostly from worn fragments of other rocks. The sedimentary rocks mask the underlying igneous and metamorphic rocks.

Which common rocks are igneous or metamorphic?

Basalt is an igneous rock formed from molten lava. Granite, another igneous rock, hardens underground. Heat and pressure turn shale and limestone (sedimentary rocks) into slate and marble (metamorphic rocks).

Basalt

Slate

Granite

Marble

Is coal a kind of rock?

Coal is a rock formed largely from the remains of such plants as ferns, horsetails, and mosses, which once grew in swampy forests. Most of the world's coal was formed in the Carboniferous period, between 345 and 280 million years ago.

How are fossils formed?

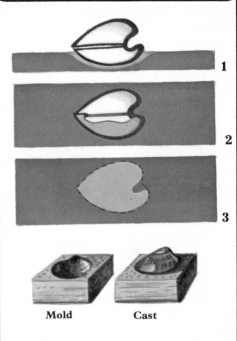

Mold   **Cast**

When a shellfish dies (1), its shell may be buried (2). Later, the shell may be dissolved away, leaving a fossil mold. Later still, the mold may be filled by a mineral, and a fossil cast is created (3).

Which are sedimentary?

Sedimentary rocks include coal and limestones, some of which formed largely from the remains of sea creatures. Other sedimentary rocks consist of such fragments as pebbles, sand, and silt. They include conglomerates, sandstones, and shale.

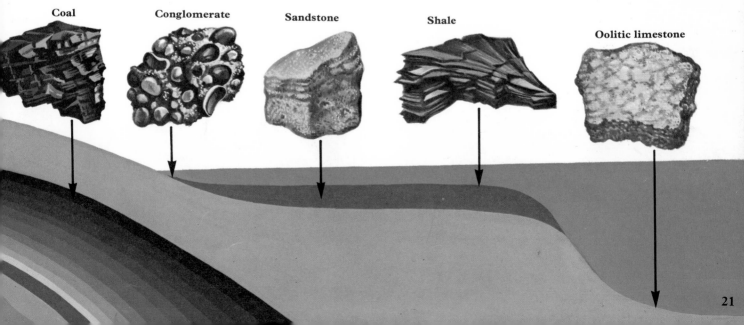

Coal   **Conglomerate**   **Sandstone**   **Shale**   **Oolitic limestone**

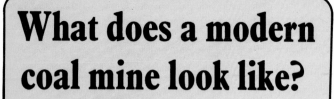

What does a modern coal mine look like?

RICHES FROM THE EARTH The Earth's crust is a storehouse of valuable substances, such as the fossil fuels (coal, oil, and natural gas) formed from the remains of once-living things. Many items used in everyday life are made from substances mined from the Earth. For example, steel products are made from iron and carbon, often combined with small amounts of chromium, manganese, and nickel. Mines also produce gold and precious stones. However, the Earth's resources are today being used up so quickly that we must protect and conserve them.

Modern coal mines are much safer places in which to work than those of the past. They are well ventilated by air shafts. And the miners are equipped with much labor-saving machinery to cut the coal and get it to the surface.

Pithead

Shaft

Cage

Air pump

Placing explosives

Cutting machine

Cutaway showing adjustable steel props supporting roof

Where are oil and natural gas found?

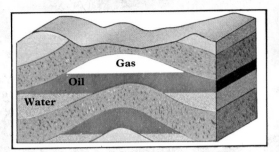

Natural gas and oil are often trapped in porous rocks (through which gases and liquids can seep) in an upfold, or *anticline*. The gas and oil cannot escape, because the porous rock is enclosed by layers of solid rock. Water often underlies the oil.

How is oil extracted from under shallow water?

Engineers build rigs in order to extract natural gas and oil from rocks beneath shallow waters, such as in the North Sea and in Lake Maracaibo, Venezuela. The rigs must be able to withstand the pounding of the waves.

What treasured substances are found in the Earth?

Gold nugget

Diamond

Ruby

Topaz

Three types of iron ore

Valuable substances in the Earth's crust include fossil fuels and metals, some of which—for example, gold—are rare. There are also such precious stones as diamonds, rubies, and sapphires, which are cut to show off their best features and made into beautiful jewelery.

How long will Earth's reserves of fuels and metals last?

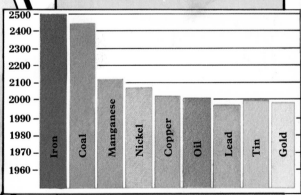

The diagram shows how long the known resources of various fuels and metals will last at present rates of consumption. The diagram does not allow for new discoveries, the re-use of existing metals, or the extraction of metals from the oceans.

Why do some places get more heat from the Sun than others?

N. Pole

Sun's rays

Sun's rays

Sun's rays

S. Pole

The Sun's rays are most concentrated around the Equator. Near the poles, they spread over a much larger land area and so they are much less effective. Another factor is that, near the poles, the Sun's rays lose a lot of their heat by passing through a greater thickness of air.

How do winds blow over the Earth?

Horse latitudes

Doldrums

Horse latitudes

The map shows the main wind systems—the polar easterlies (black arrows), the south-westerlies (white), and the trade winds (red). In general, winds blow from areas of high pressure, such as the horse latitudes and the polar regions, toward areas of low pressure, such as the doldrums.

CLIMATE AND WEATHER The Earth is a varied place, with many climatic regions, ranging from the icy poles to the hot equatorial lands. The climate of a region is a description of the typical or average weather. Weather is the day-to-day condition of the air. Weather features, such as temperature, air pressure, winds, rain and so on, are measured at weather stations. Weather forecasters try to predict the future weather from such information.

What instruments are used by weather forecasters?

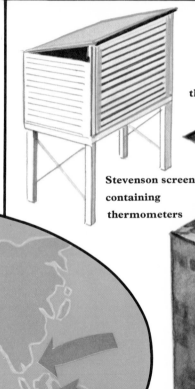

Anemometer

Soil thermometer

Weather vane

Stevenson screen containing thermometers

Sunshine recorder

Rain gauge

At weather stations, meteorologists measure wind speeds and directions with *anemometers*, rainfall in *rain gauges*, and air temperatures with *thermometers* shaded inside a screen. They measure air pressure with *barometers* or *barographs*, and sunshine with *sunshine recorders*.

Are there distinct climatic regions?

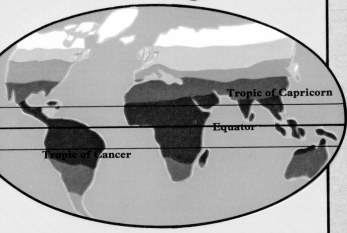

Temperature and rainfall mostly determine the five main climatic types: polar climates (white), cold forest climates (yellow), mid-latitude temperate climates (bright green), dry deserts (dark green), and tropical rainy climates (brown). In some classifications there is a mountain climate, similar to polar, but due to altitude.

What does a weather map tell us?

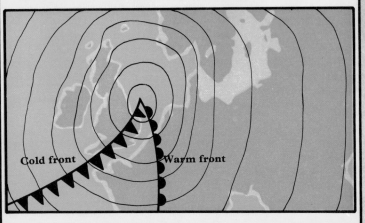

The lines on weather maps that resemble contours are *isobars*. They link places with the same atmospheric pressure. Low-pressure air systems often contain warm and cold fronts, areas associated with rain.

Where does the moisture in the atmosphere come from?

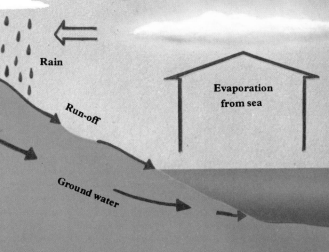

The water cycle brings a regular supply of fresh water to land areas. The Sun's heat evaporates water from the sea. Water vapor (a gas) rises and forms clouds. The clouds are blown over the land and the water vapor falls as rain or snow. The water then drains back into the sea.

WEATHER AND WATER MOLD THE LAND

The land is always changing. Weathering is one of the main ways in which the land is changed. It occurs, for example, when ice shatters rocks. And, in deserts, rapid changes in temperature cause rocks to peel away. Weathering also includes chemical action, such as the wearing away of limestone by rainwater. After weathering has broken up or loosened rock, other natural forces take over. In wet regions, the chief agent of erosion is running water.

Do mountains and cliffs wear away?

Rocks may be shattered by weathering. This often occurs when water fills cracks in the rocks. When the water freezes, the ice widens the cracks until, finally, the rock is split apart. The heaps of broken rock that pile up at the bottom of mountain slopes are called *scree*.

How does rainwater dissolve rock?

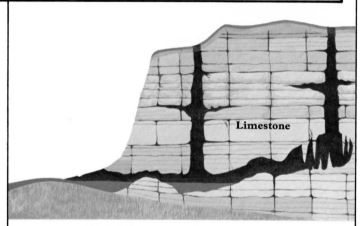

Limestone

Rainwater dissolves carbon dioxide from the air, making it a weak acid. This acid reacts with the hard rock limestone, slowly wearing it away. The water seeps through the limestone, dissolving away huge caves. The water finally reappears at a spring at the base of the limestone.

What is meant by the "water table"?

Rainwater seeps through the soil and rocks into the *zone of saturation*. There, every pore and crack in the rocks is filled with water. The top of this zone is the *water table*. Lakes and swamps occur where the water table meets the surface. Wells are drilled down to the water table.

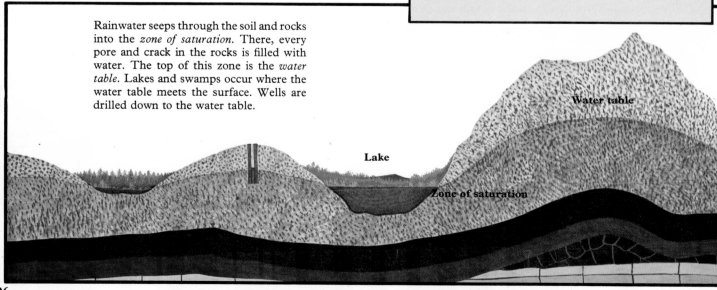

Water table

Lake

Zone of saturation

What causes springs?

Spring

Aquifer

Springs occur where water-bearing rock layers, called *aquifers*, reach the surface. Aquifers are often enclosed, above and below, by solid, impervious rocks, through which water cannot seep. Springs are the sources of many rivers. Other rivers flow from lakes or melting glaciers.

Youthful stage

Meander

Mature stage

Ox-bow lake

What are the main features of a river's course?

Rivers in mountain areas are said to be *youthful*. They flow quickly and wear out deep valleys. As the slope decreases, rivers enter their vigorous *mature stage*. In *old age*, rivers flow slowly across flat plains, carrying sediment into the sea.

Old-age stage

Delta

How are waterfalls formed?

Hard rock

Softer rock

Waterfalls usually occur at places where hard rocks resist river erosion and softer rocks, beneath the hard rock, are undercut. Occasionally, slabs of hard rock are undermined and crash down. In this way, waterfalls are always retreating.

What does a glacier look like?

Glaciers are rivers of ice that flow down valleys in mountainous regions and around the poles. Their surfaces are often littered with weathered rock. Rocks also become frozen within the ice and in its bottom and sides. This rock is called *moraine*.

THE WORK OF ICE AND WIND In cold regions, ice is a major agent of erosion. Ice sheets cover most of Antarctica and Greenland, and there are many glaciers in the mountains of temperate lands. Glacier ice forms from compacted snow. Glaciers are long tongues of ice that flow downhill. Jagged rocks, frozen in the ice, scrape over the land. In dry deserts, winds are the main force of erosion.

What effect do glaciers have on highland regions?

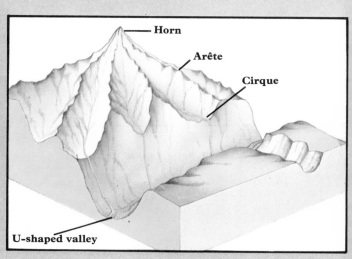

Glaciers deepen valleys into a U-shape. Ice also wears out armchair-shaped hollows, called *cirques*, which are separated by knife-edged ridges, called *arêtes*.

What effect do they have on lowlands?

When glaciers reach the warmer lowlands, they start to melt. Streams carry some of the moraine and spread it over the land. Other features, such as *terminal moraines*, are ridges of moraine dumped by the glacier.

What effect does the wind have on deserts?

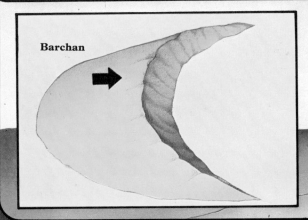

Barchan

"Sand-blasting"

In dry deserts, winds blow sand into dunes, such as the crescent-shaped *bar-chans*. Wind-blown sand acts like a natural sand-blaster. It cuts into the lower parts of rocks, carving them into top-heavy shapes, standing on small stems—like mushrooms.

What is the largest hot desert?

The world's largest hot desert is the Sahara, in northern Africa. It was not always a desert. About 6,000 years ago, it was a grassland. But it has gradually dried up, and it is probably still spreading southward, because of severe droughts.

Sahara

What is an oasis like?

Oases are the fertile parts of deserts. They sometimes occur when underground water-bearing rocks reach the surface in hollows. Large oases support many people, who grow dates and other crops. Small oases are watering places for desert nomads.

Water-bearing rock

How high can waves in the ocean rise?

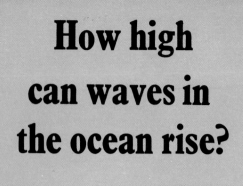

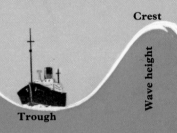

Crest

Wave height

Trough

The height of a wave is the vertical distance between the trough and the crest. The highest recorded wave was 112 feet (34 m) high. A sailor on board the USS *Ramapo* in the Pacific Ocean measured it during a gale in 1933.

THE WORK OF THE SEA The most familiar movements of the sea are waves. But waves do not move the water across the open sea. They are caused mainly by winds. When a wave passes through the sea, the water particles move around in a circle—not horizontally. Watch a corked bottle in the sea. It stays in the same place unless the wind catches it. Other movements of the sea are tides and currents. Along coasts, the sea molds the land.

What are neap tides and spring tides?

Spring tides, the highest tides, occur when the Earth, Moon, and Sun are in a straight line. The gravitational force of the Moon and Sun on ocean water is then combined. Low *neap tides* occur when the Earth, Moon, and Sun form a right angle.

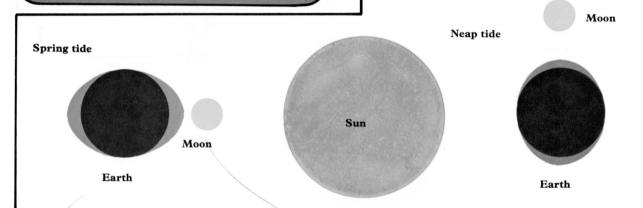

Spring tide

Neap tide

Moon

Sun

Earth

Moon

Earth

What are the main ocean currents?

Currents shown in dark brown are warm, those in dark blue are cold.

The oceans' waters are constantly mixed by currents. Surface currents are caused chiefly by winds. The density of the water is also important. Density varies according to the temperature and saltiness of the water.

Does the sea carve away the land?

During storms, waves hurl pebbles and rocks at cliffs, creating caves (1). Caves may be worn into both sides of a headland (2). The caves may unite in a natural arch (3). When the cave collapses, a stack remains isolated in the sea (4).

Does it ever create new land?

Material worn from the land may be swept out to sea or carried along coasts by currents and waves. The material may be dumped in long ridges, called *spits*. Sometimes, it forms a bar across a bay, sealing off the bay from the sea.

A-Z of the Earth

A

abyss The name for the deep parts of the ocean beyond the continental slope.

air *See* ATMOSPHERE.

Alps A high, fold-mountain range in south-central Europe. The highest peak is Mont Blanc, in France. It is 15,781 feet (4,810 m) above sea level.

Amazon River Mainly in Brazil, South America, it is the world's second longest river, about 4,000 miles (6,440 km) long.

anemometer An instrument used at weather stations to measure the speed, and often the direction, of the wind.

anticline An up-fold or arch of rock layers caused by pressure.

arête A knife-edged ridge between two armchair-shaped depressions called *cirques*. Arêtes are formed by ice action in mountain regions.

artesian well A kind of well in which the underground water-bearing rock is tilted. The trapped water is under pressure and it gushes to the surface.

atmosphere The mixture of gases that surrounds the Earth—mainly oxygen (20.95%), nitrogen (78.09%), and argon (0.93%). Tiny amounts of various other gases also occur. It also contains water vapor and dust. The atmosphere becomes thinner the higher you travel.

avalanche A mass of snow and ice, often containing much rock, which crashes down mountainsides. They may be started by thaws or by sudden, loud sounds.

axis An imaginary line joining the North Pole, the center of the Earth, and the South Pole. The Earth rotates on its axis once every 24 hours.

B

bar A ridge of sand and shingle that runs parallel to the coast or from a headland across a bay or estuary.

barchan A crescent-shaped sand dune.

barometer Any instrument used to measure air pressure. One kind consists of a sealed glass tube containing mercury, which is suspended upside-down in a bath of mercury. As the air pressure increases, it pushes down on the mercury, and the mercury in the tube rises.

basalt An igneous rock, formed when burning-hot lava cools and solidifies.

batholiths Enormous dome-shaped masses of igneous rock. They are formed underground when molten magma hardens.

block mountains Mountains formed when a large block of land is pushed upward between faults (cracks) in the Earth's crust.

boulder clay The name for material dumped on the land by glaciers. It contains rocks embedded in extremely fine, ground-down sand and clay.

C

canyon A river-worn valley that has extremely steep sides.

Carlsbad Caverns A cave system in New Mexico. They contain the world's largest cave. It is called the Big Room, and is about 4,000 feet (1,220 m) long, nearly 328 feet (100 m) high, and about 656 feet (200 m) wide.

cave A hollow beneath the Earth's surface. Some caves occur in cliffs on the coast or in hardened lava. But most occur in limestone rocks, which are dissolved away by water containing carbon dioxide.

chalk A white or greyish limestone. Many kinds of chalk consist largely of the remains of once-living organisms. Note that blackboard "chalk" consists of a quite different material, gypsum.

cirques Armchair-shaped depressions in mountain regions. These steep-sided, round hollows often contain lakes, called *tarns*, which were worn out by ice.

climate The average, or typical, weather of a place or region.

cloud A mass of water droplets or ice crystals in the air. There are two main kinds of clouds. Some, such as *stratus*, form in layers or sheets. Others, such as *cumulus*, form in huge heaps.

coal A rock formed from the remains of decayed plants.

conglomerate A sedimentary rock containing rounded pebbles embedded in finer material. This rock formed at the mouths of rivers, where the heavy pebbles were dropped in the shallow water, while fine silt and mud were swept out to sea.

continent The name for large land-masses and the islands that lie around them. They are as follows:

Asia	16,988,000 sq mi
Africa	11,506,000 sq mi
North America	9,390,000 sq mi
South America	6,795,000 sq mi
Antarctica	5,500,000 sq mi
Europe	3,745,000 sq mi
Oceania (including Australia)	2,968,000 sq mi

continental drift The name for the movement of continents around the face of the Earth. According to the theory of continental drift, all the continents were once joined together, but they split apart and drifted to their present positions in the last 200 million years.

continental shelf The shallow sea bed around continents. It ends where the continental slope begins. The edge of the continental shelf is the true edge of the continents.

continental slope The steep slope joining the continental shelf to the abyss.

convection currents The type of current that occurs when a flame is placed under a pan of water. Particles of water expand and rise. At the surface, they spread sideways, cool, and finally sink to the bottom. Similar currents occur in the air. For example, at the Equator, warm air rises and spreads north and south, finally sinking again in the horse latitudes. Convection currents also occur in the rocks of the Earth's mantle, under the crust, where the spreading of the rock under the crust causes continental drift.

core The Earth's core has a diameter of 4,300 miles (6,920 km). The inner core is solid, but the outer core consists of molten, liquid rock.

crevasse A deep crack in a glacier or ice sheet.

crust The Earth's crust is a thin shell about 4 miles (6 km) thick under the oceans and up to 37–43 miles (60–70 km) thick under continental mountain ranges.

currents, ocean Ocean water is moved by currents. Winds cause most surface ocean currents, but some are caused by differences in density, resulting from differing temperatures of differing amounts of salt in the water.

D

day The time taken by the Earth to revolve once on its axis.

Dead Sea An extremely salty lake between Israel and Jordan. Its shore is the world's lowest place on land—1,289 feet (393 m) below sea level.

delta An area of land formed at the mouth of a river from sediments dropped there by the river.

desert A dry area, usually with an average of less than 10 inches (250 mm) of rain per year.

dinosaur The name for a large group of animals that lived in the Mesozoic era between about 225 and 65 million years ago. Our knowledge of them comes from fossils, and no one knows for sure why they died out.

doldrums The zone around the Equator in which the trade winds blow. The zone is marked by calm weather.

drumlin An egg-shaped hill formed from boulder clay deposited by ice.

dune A mound or ridge of sand.

E

earthquakes Sudden movements of the land along faults. Earthquake tremors may cause great damage.

Equator An imaginary line around the Earth, half-way between the North and South Poles.

equinoxes Two days every year when the Sun is directly overhead at the Equator. The *spring equinox* occurs on about March 21 and the *autumnal equinox* on about September 23. Equinox means "equal night." At the equinoxes, everywhere on Earth has a 12-hour day and night.

erosion The wearing away of the land by weathering, running water, ice, sea waves, and winds.

esker A ridge of ice-worn material formed by a stream that once flowed under an ice sheet or glacier.

estuary The part of the mouth of a river that is affected by tides.

Everest Mountain on the Nepal–Tibet border in the Himalayas. The world's highest peak, it is 29,028 feet (8,848 m) above sea level.

F

fault A break or crack in rocks, along which the rocks have moved.

fiord or **fjord** A deep, U-shaped valley worn out by a glacier, but now filled by the sea.

flood plain A flat area that is often flooded when an old-age river overflows its banks.

fold mountains Formed by lateral (sideways) pressure, which pushes rocks upwards in great loops or folds.

fossils Evidence in rocks of once-living animals and plants.

G

glaciation The action of ice on the land. The ice molds the rocks, producing distinctive landforms.

glacier A mass of ice that moves downward from its source in a mountain area along a valley.

Grand Canyon A deep valley worn out by the Colorado River in the southwestern United States. It is about 200 miles (320 km) long, up to 1 mile (1·6 km) deep, and 2 to 18 miles (3 to 29 km) wide.

granite A common igneous rock, formed when magma solidifies underground.

Greenwich Mean Time The standard time at the Greenwich Observatory, London, which lies on longitude 0°. Time zones are measured east and west of Greenwich.

ground water Water that seeps through the soil and the rocks that lie beneath the Earth's surface.

H

Hawaiian volcanoes These do not erupt explosively, but emit streams of molten lava, which flow great distances. Because they do not explode, they are said to be "quiet" volcanoes. Hawaiian volcanoes resemble upturned saucers.

Himalayas The world's highest mountain range. These fold mountains include Everest, the world's highest peak.

horn A pointed mountain peak, worn away by glaciation.

horse latitudes Areas of high air pressure around 30° North and 30° South. Trade winds and westerlies blow outward from the horse latitudes.

horst A block of land raised up as a ridge between faults.

I-K

iceberg A floating mass of ice that has broken away from an ice sheet or glacier. Only about nine-tenths of an iceberg appears above the waves.

igneous rocks Rocks formed when molten magma solidifies either on the surface or underground.

International Date Line A line around 180° longitude, on the opposite side of the Earth to the prime meridian (0° longitude). East of the prime meridian, 180° represents a *gain* of 12 hours. West of the prime meridian, 180° represents a *loss* of 12 hours. Hence the time difference on either side of the International Date Line is 24 hours, or 1 day.

Krakatoa A volcanic island between Java and Sumatra that exploded in 1883. It was the biggest explosion of modern times.

L

landslides Movements of rock and soil down steep slopes. They may be caused by heavy rain or by earthquakes.

latitude Lines drawn on maps parallel to the equator (0° latitude) are called *lines of latitude* or *parallels*. Other lines, at right-angles to lines of latitude and passing through both poles, are called *lines of longitude*.

lava Molten rock, or magma, which appears on the Earth's surface.

limestone A common sedimentary rock, formed mostly of calcium carbonate. Chalk is the purest form.

longitude *See* LATITUDE.

M

magma Molten rock that may erupt as lava or harden underground.

magnetic poles The Earth is like a giant magnet. Like all magnets, it has two magnetic poles. These lie near the geographical poles.

mantle The section of the Earth between the thin crust and the core.

marble A metamorphic rock formed when great heat and pressure *metamorphose* (change) limestone.

Mauna Kea A Hawaiian volcano, the world's highest mountain measured from the sea bed. It has a height of 33,474 feet (10,203 m), but only 13,796 feet (4,205 m) is above sea level.

meander A bend in a river.

meridian A line of longitude.

metamorphic rocks Rocks that have been *metamorphosed*, changed by heat, pressure, or chemical action.

moraine Rocks and clay deposited by ice sheets and glaciers.

mountains They may be volcanic or formed by lateral pressure (fold mountains) or by the raising up of land between faults (horsts and block mountains).

N

nappe A fold in rocks that has been sheared and pushed forwards, masking the rocks beneath it.

natural gas Probably formed from the remains of once-living organisms. It is found trapped in porous rocks, often above deposits of petroleum (oil).

Nile The world's longest river. It flows 4,415 miles (6,670 km) through northeastern Africa.

nuée ardente A feature of some volcanic eruptions. The term means "glowing cloud" and, when the volcano explodes, it emits a cloud of hot gases, steam, and fragments of ash which rolls downhill, burning all in its path.

O

oasis A place in a desert where there is surface water. It may be a small pond or a large area, such as the Nile valley in Egypt.

Old Faithful The name of a geyser in Yellowstone National Park. On the average, it erupts a jet of hot water and steam once every 65 minutes.

ox-bow lake Some rivers straighten their courses by cutting through the necks of meanders (bends). The former meander is then cut off and remains, for a while, as an ox-bow lake.

P

Pangaea The name for an ancient continent that, about 200 million years ago, consisted of all of our present continents joined together. But Pangaea split up and the parts moved to their present positions because of continental drift.

parallel A line of latitude.

Pelée, Mount A volcano on Martinique, a West Indian island. It erupted in 1902 and a huge *nuée ardente* (glowing cloud) destroyed the town of St. Pierre.

plateau The name for a mostly level upland region.

poles The points at the end of the Earth's axis—the North Pole and the South Pole. The magnetic poles are near the geographical poles.

Pompeii A former Roman town near the Bay of Naples, Italy. In AD 79, the nearby volcano, Mt. Vesuvius, exploded. A cloud of hot pumice and ash rained down on Pompeii, which remained buried and forgotten for hundreds of years.

prime meridian The name for 0° longitude, which passes from the North Pole, through Greenwich Observatory, London, to the South Pole. The line was fixed by international agreement in 1884.

R

rain gauge An instrument used at weather stations to measure precipitation (rain, snow, hail, and so on).

rift valley A valley formed when a block of land sinks down between faults. They are often deep and steep-sided, and contain many lakes.

S

Sahara In northern Africa, it is the world's largest hot desert. It covers about 3 million square miles (7.8 million square kilometers).

San Francisco earthquake Occurred in 1906 when there was a sudden shift along the nearby San Andreas fault. Fires caused by broken gas pipes and electrical short circuits destroyed much of San Francisco. Scientists are now predicting another earthquake in the area.

Santorini (or **Thera**) A Greek island where, in about 1470 BC, the world's greatest volcanic explosion occured. A *tsunami* (ocean wave) triggered by the explosion may have destroyed the ancient Minoan civilization in the eastern Mediterranean.

scree Broken, weathered rock that piles up at the foot of mountain slopes.

seasons The seasons occur because the Earth's axis is tilted. As a result, as the Earth orbits the Sun, the Northern and Southern Hemispheres are tilted toward and away from the Sun.

sedimentary rocks Formed from eroded rock fragments; or from the remains of once-living organisms; or from chemicals precipitated from water.

seismograph An instrument used to record and measure the intensity of earthquakes.

sink hole A pit in a limestone outcrop. It was dissolved out by rain water and it leads down to the caves below.

slate A hard metamorphic rock formed when soft shale is subjected to pressure and heat.

solar system The name for all the bodies, including the Earth, that orbit around the Sun.

solstices Two days every year when the overhead Sun reaches its northernmost and southernmost points. The summer solstice, with the Sun overhead at the Tropic of Cancer, is on about June 21. The winter solstice, when the Sun is overhead at the southern Tropic of Capricorn, occurs on about December 21.

spit A ridge of worn material deposited by waves and currents in the sea.

spring A flow of ground water on to the surface, where it may form a stream.

stack An isolated pillar of rock in the sea, which was cut off from the land by wave action.

stalactite A long, icicle-like growth of rock from the roof of a limestone cave. It is formed from calcite precipitated from dripping water.

stalagmite A pillar of rock that grows upward from the floor of a limestone cave.

sunshine recorder An instrument used to measure the number of hours of sunshine that occur each day.

T

thermometer An instrument for measuring temperatures.

tides The twice-daily rise and fall of sea level. They are caused by the gravitational pull of the Moon and Sun on the Earth's ocean waters.

time zone A region that has the same standard time. The world is split up into time zones, based mainly on longitude.

trade winds Winds that blow toward the Equator from the horse latitudes. In the Northern Hemisphere, they blow from the north-east to the south-west. In the Southern Hemisphere, they blow from the south-east to the north-west.

tsunami A destructive ocean wave caused by earthquakes or volcanic explosions. In the open sea, they are low but fast-moving waves. As they near land, the water piles up. The record height of a tsunami is 220 feet (67 m).

UV

U-shaped valley A steep-sided, flat-bottomed valley worn out by a glacier.

Vesuvius A volcano in southern Italy, which erupted explosively in AD 79 and buried the town of Pompeii. Most eruptions since AD 79, including the last in 1944, have been accompanied by lava flows.

W

water cycle The way in which water constantly circulates from the oceans to the land and back again.

waterfall A vertical fall of water in a river's course.

water table A surface, underground, below which the rocks are saturated with water.

weather The day-to-day condition of the air, including its temperature, the amount of moisture in it, and so on.

weathering The wearing away of rocks by the action of weather, such as the freezing of water, which splits rocks open, or the dissolving action of rain water (a weak acid) on some rocks.

weather vanes Used to measure wind directions.

well A hole dug down to the water table to obtain water.

westerlies Winds that blow polewards from the horse latitudes. In the Northern Hemisphere, they are called the south-westerlies. In the Southern Hemisphere, they are the north-westerlies.

winds Movements of air masses.

Y

year The time taken by the Earth to orbit the Sun—365 days, 5 hours, 48 minutes, and 46 seconds. Calendar years have 365 days, but we have leap years to make up for the extra time.

Index

Lerner Publications Company
241 First Avenue North, Minneapolis, Minnesota 55401